I0473233

Volume 5 of the Inspired Art Coloring Books Series

A lot of my art is inspired by my environments. I like asking people what kind of animals they like, places I hang out at, or seeing a flowering tree. The world is an amazing place. I hope that you find my images as beautiful as I do, while creating them.

Depending on your background, culture, mind set, you might see something completely different within each image. My art style was created over 25 years ago, inspired by the old method of creating silk screens. It is amazing to me that we can create such wonderful images out of pieces. That our minds can connect individual lines and merge them into these wonderful pieces of art. As I developed my style, it became how I say the energy and flow of things. An underlying base of life. People see many different cultural and artistic influences from around the world in my art. It makes my heart warm when I hear all the different things people see in my style.

In some of my images the negative space is the focus of the drawing, so when you are coloring don't limit yourself to only coloring in the lines. There is no wrong way to color. Let the colors flow how it feels right to you.

Some people don't see what I intended the image to be seen and instead find wonderful things I didn't see until they pointed them out to me.

Each page can be cut out and framed so you can display your colored creations.

I have included a page at the end of the book to test how your crayons, markers, pens, pencils, and any other medium you wish to use for bleed and look.

Because of the paper weight, colored pencils are recommended. Markers will need a sheet of cardstock or a few pieces of paper under the page you are coloring to prevent possible bleed-thru onto the next art page.

Feel free to visit my Author's page to see more of my books.

Thanks
Brian Scott

ISBN: 9781072098539

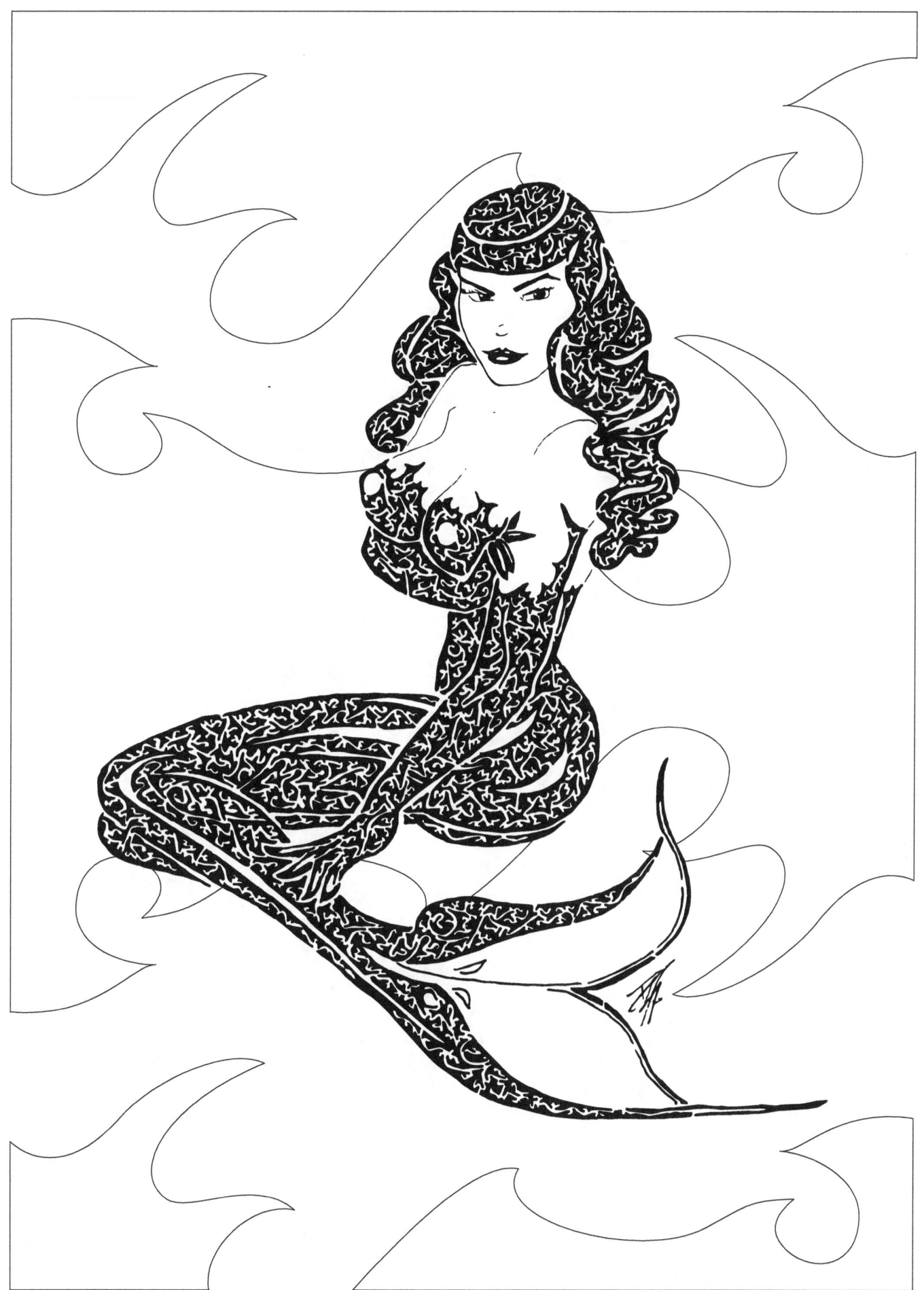

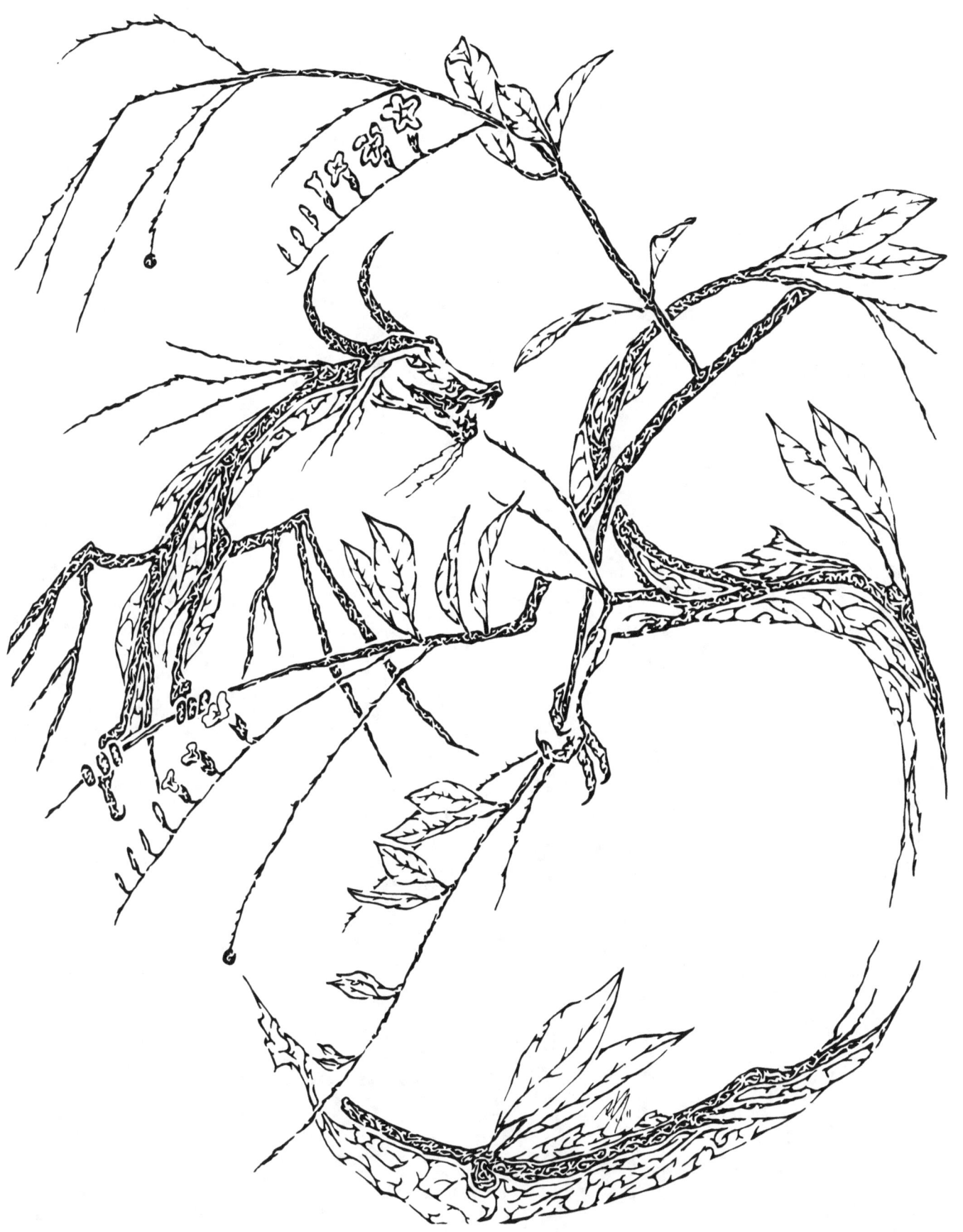

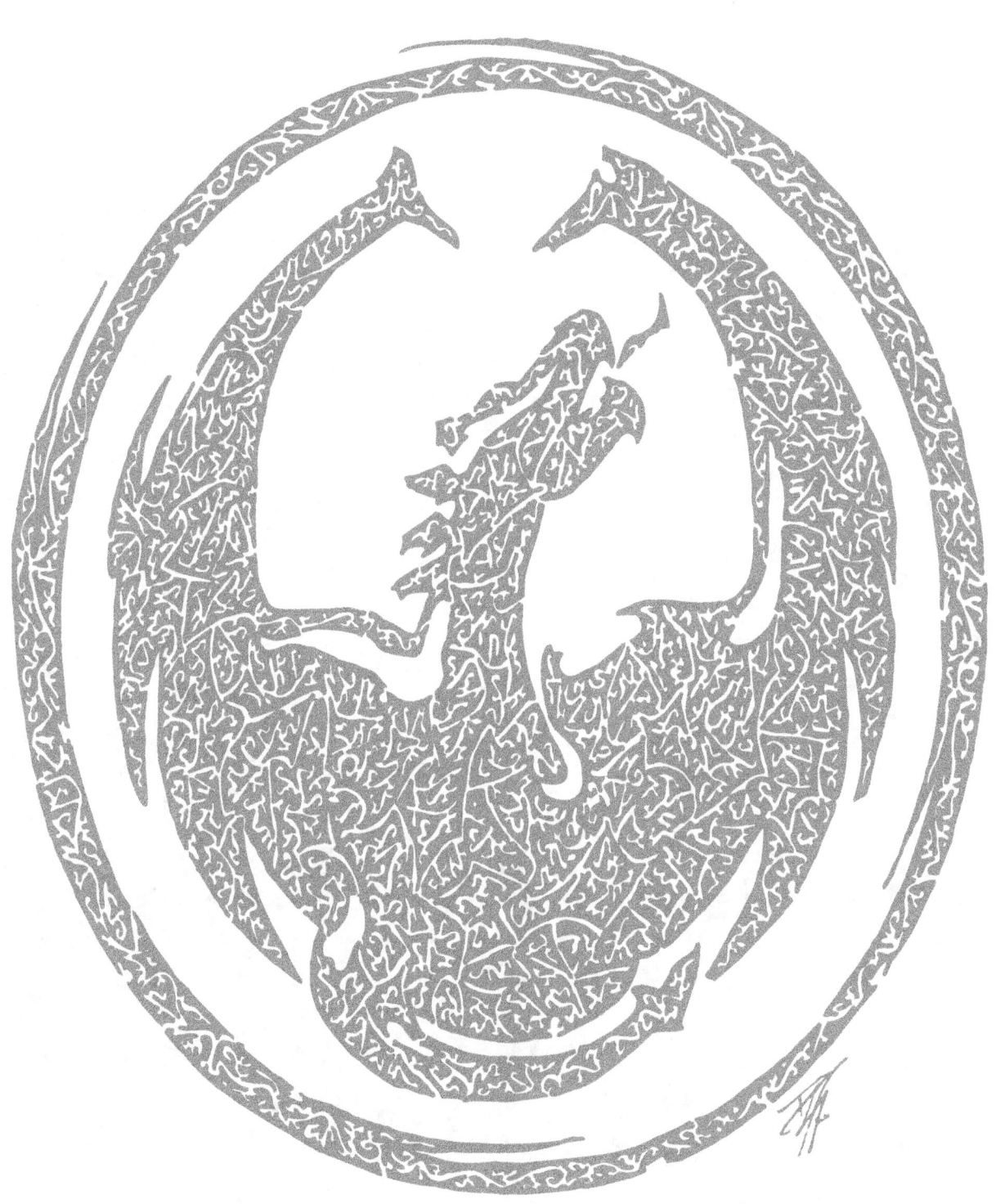

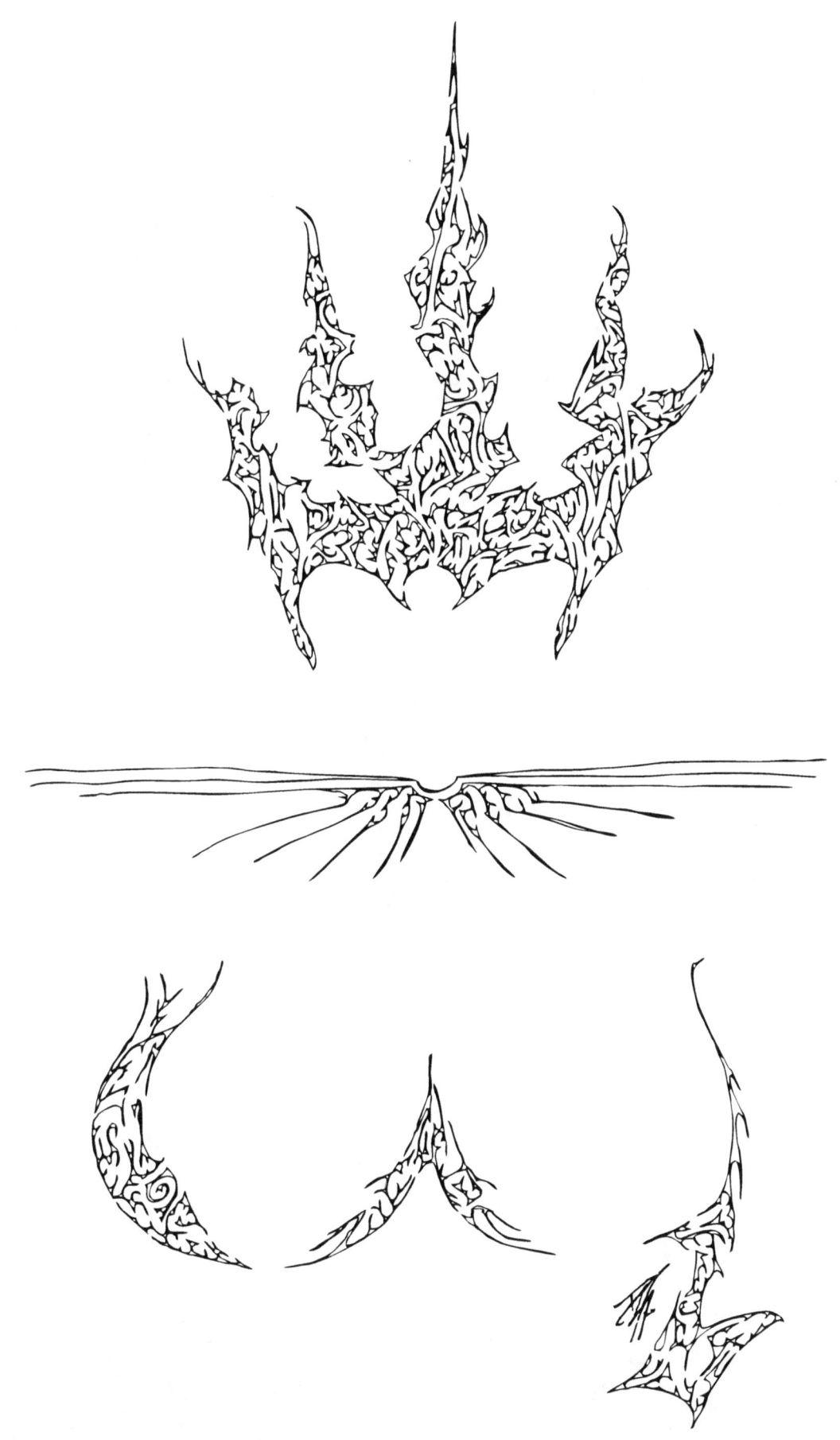

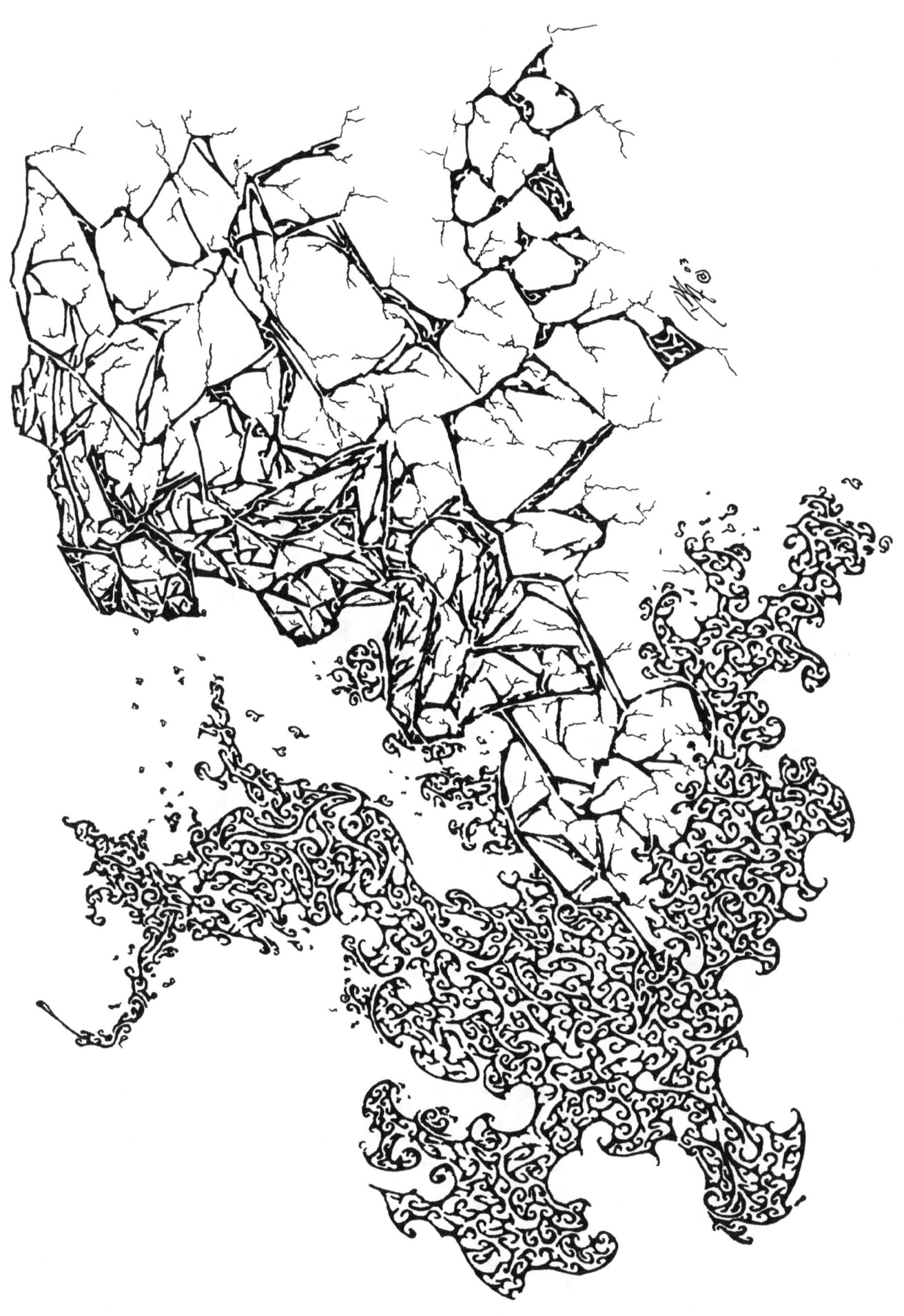

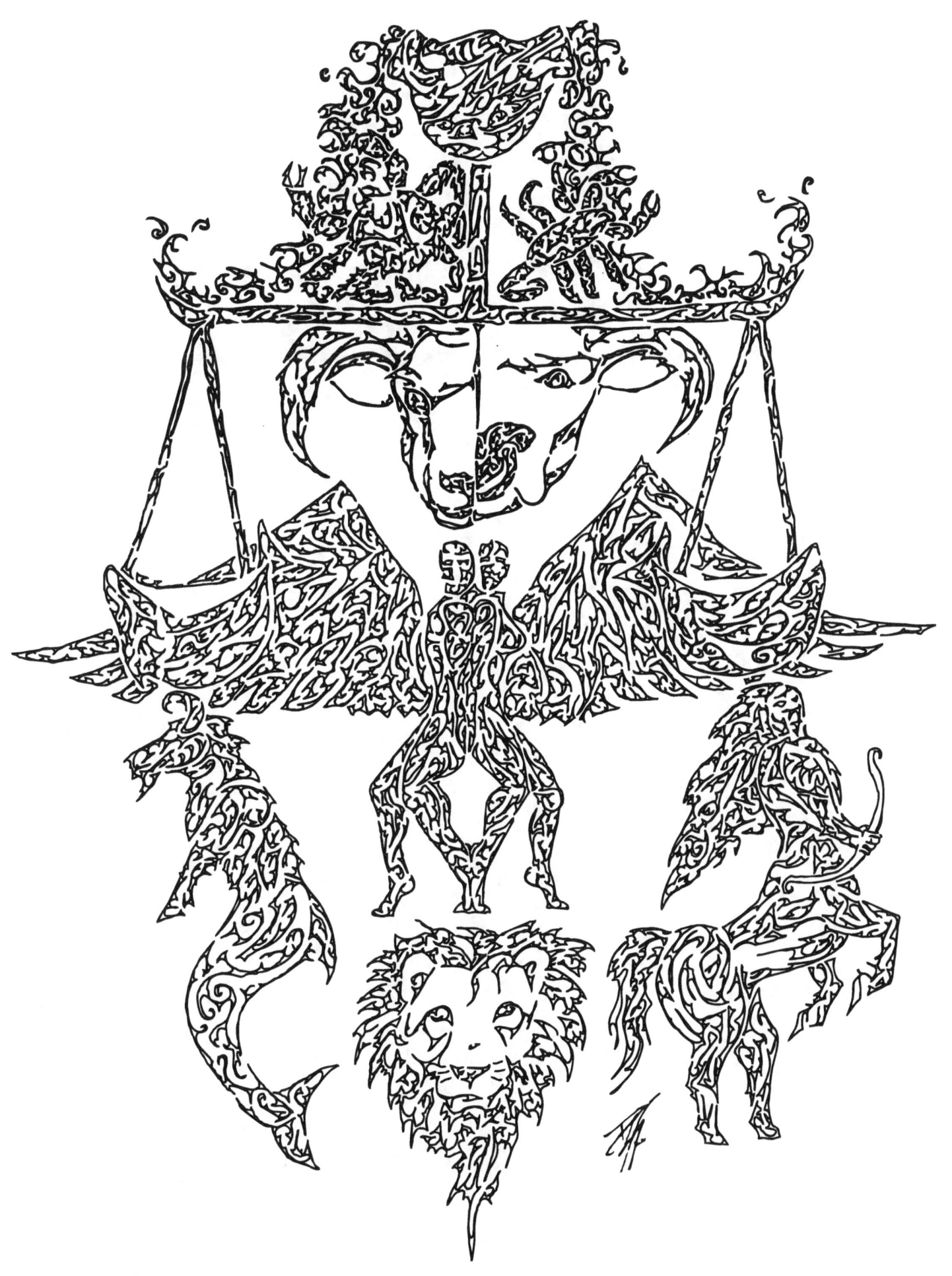

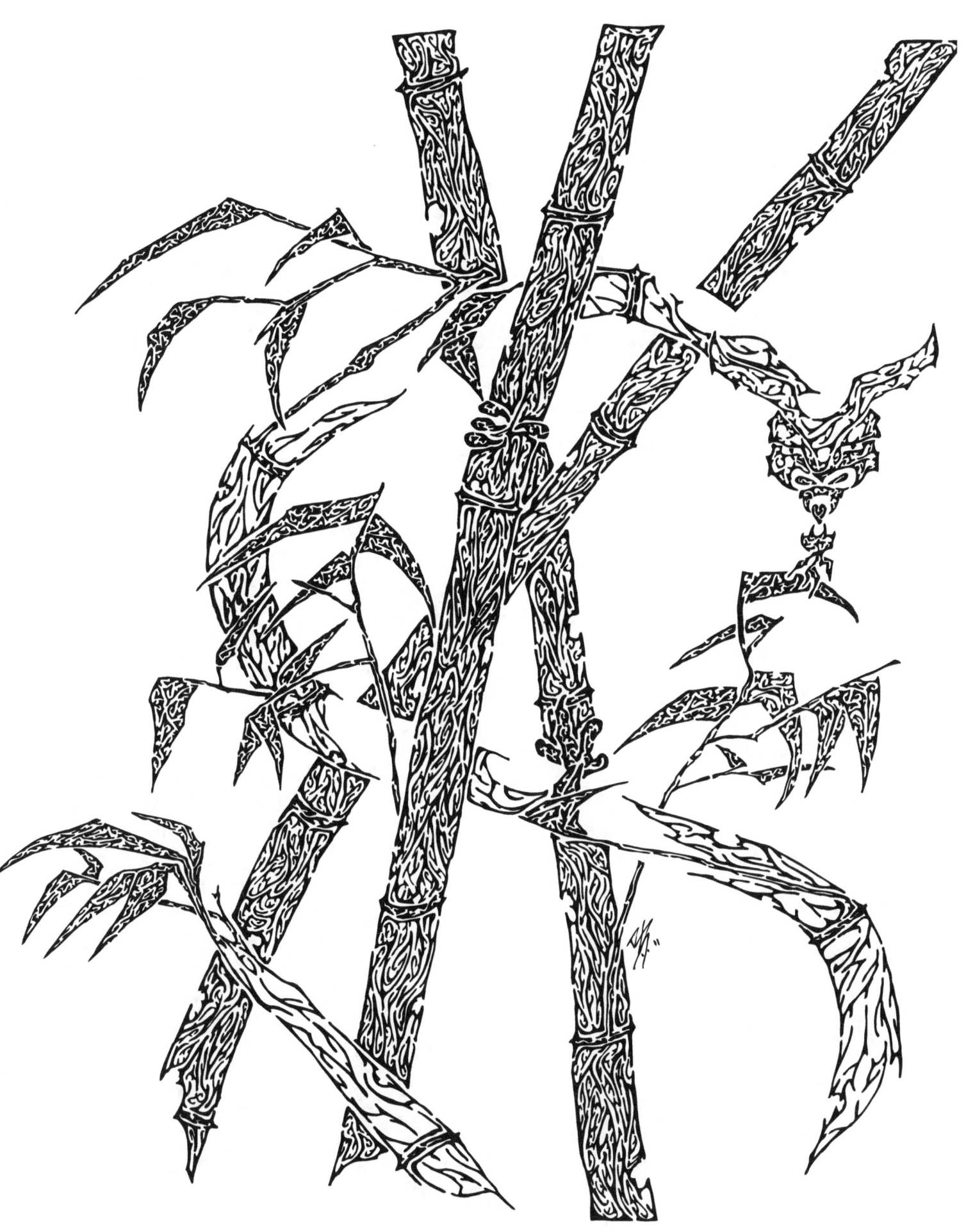

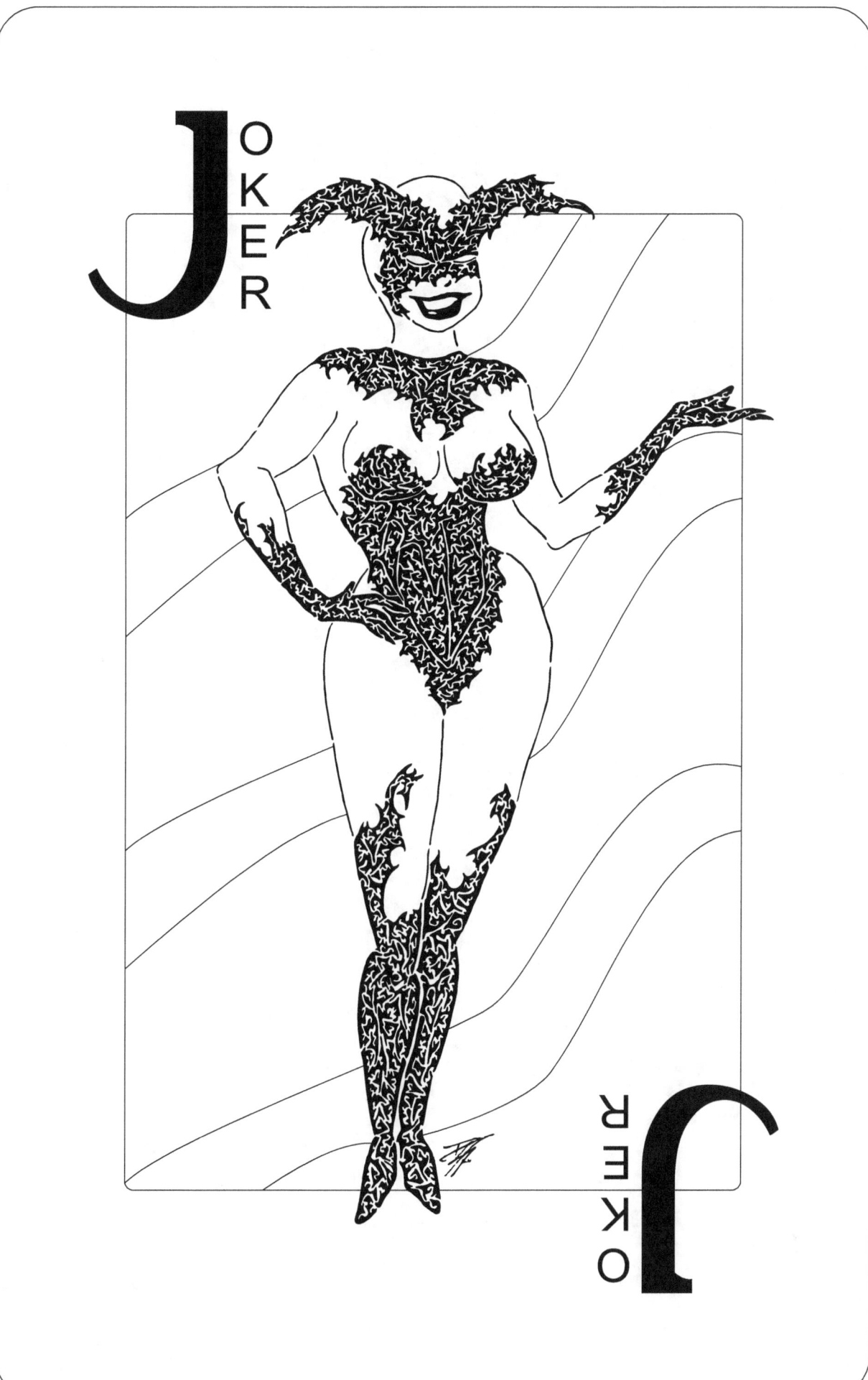

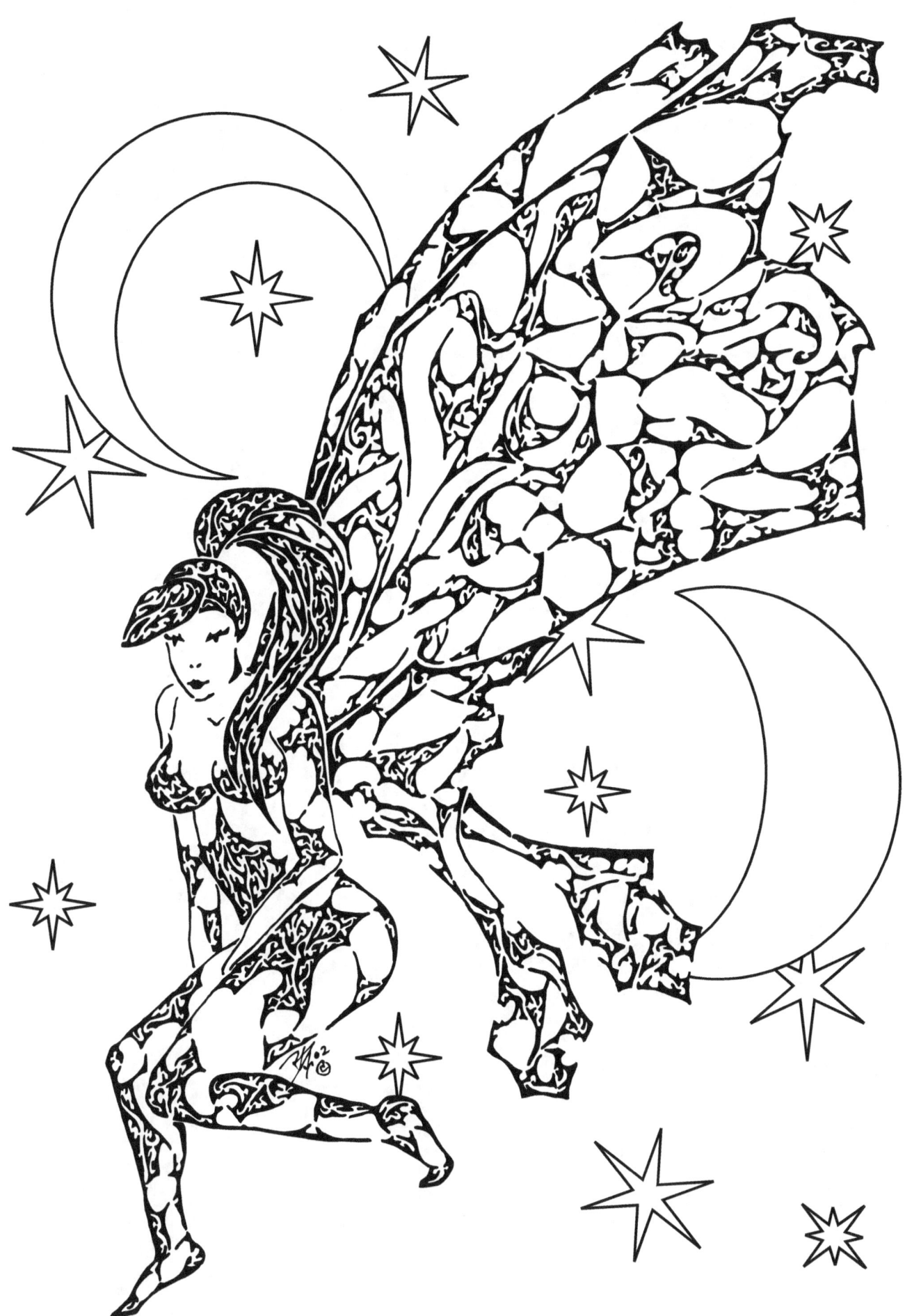

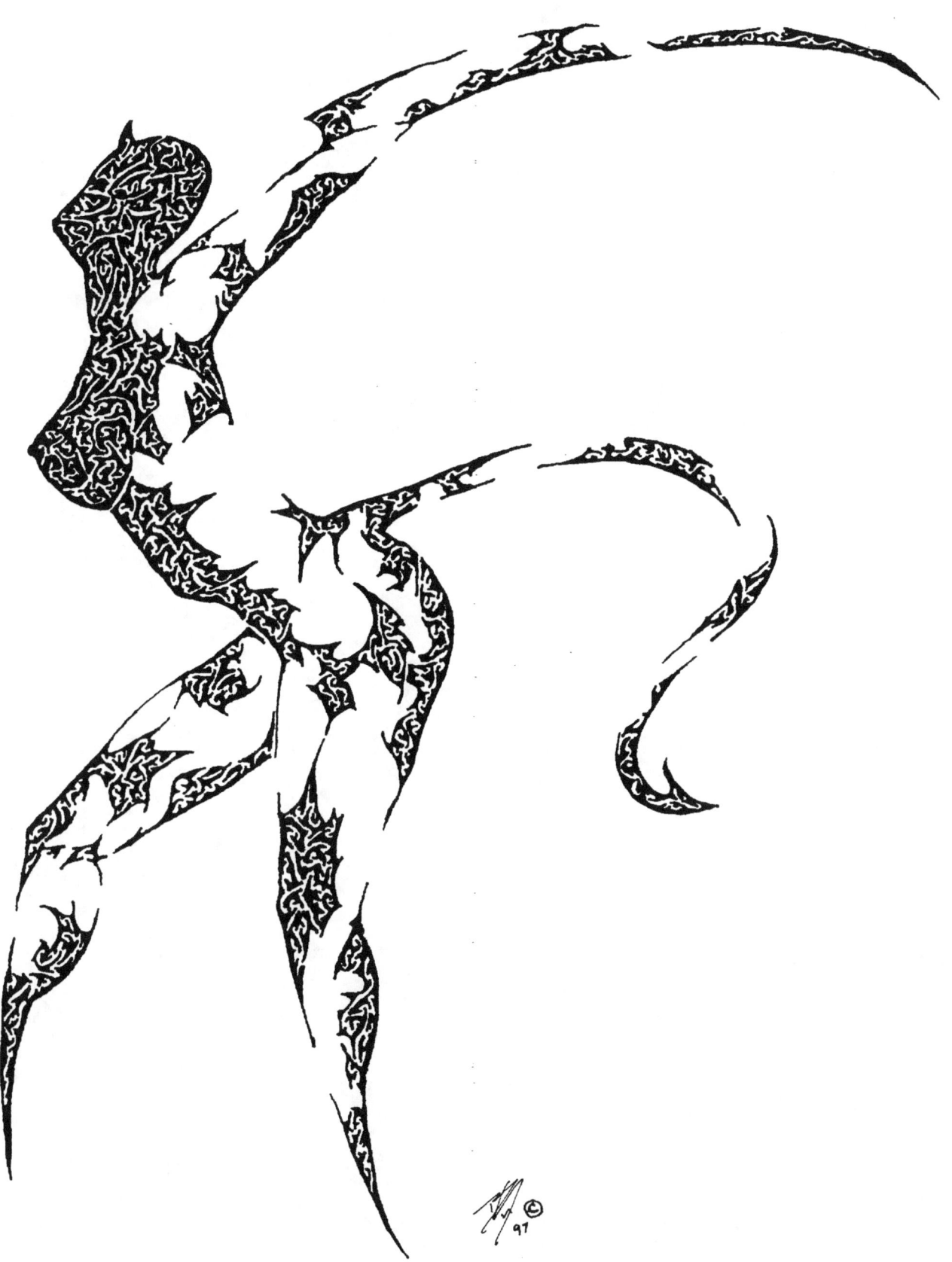

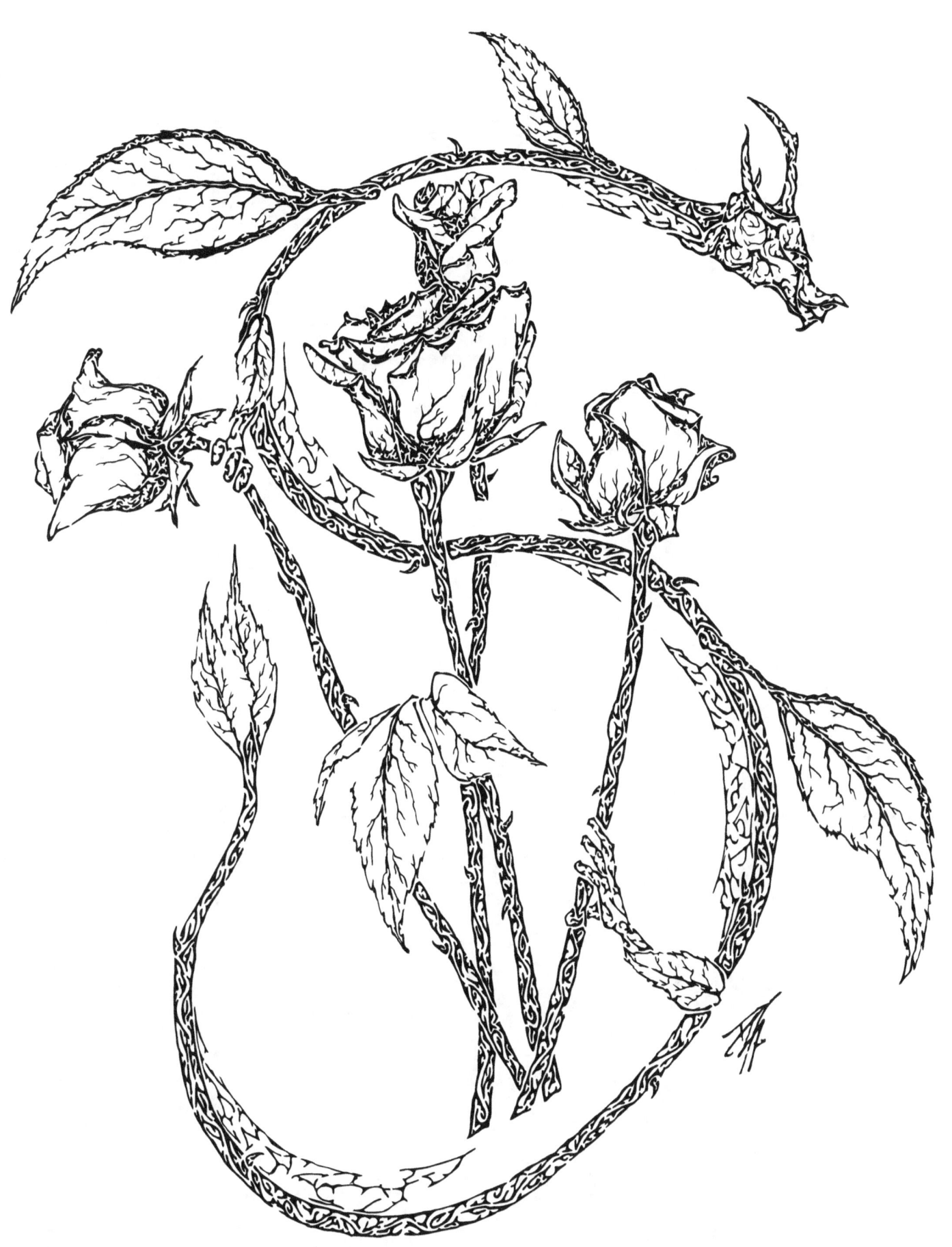

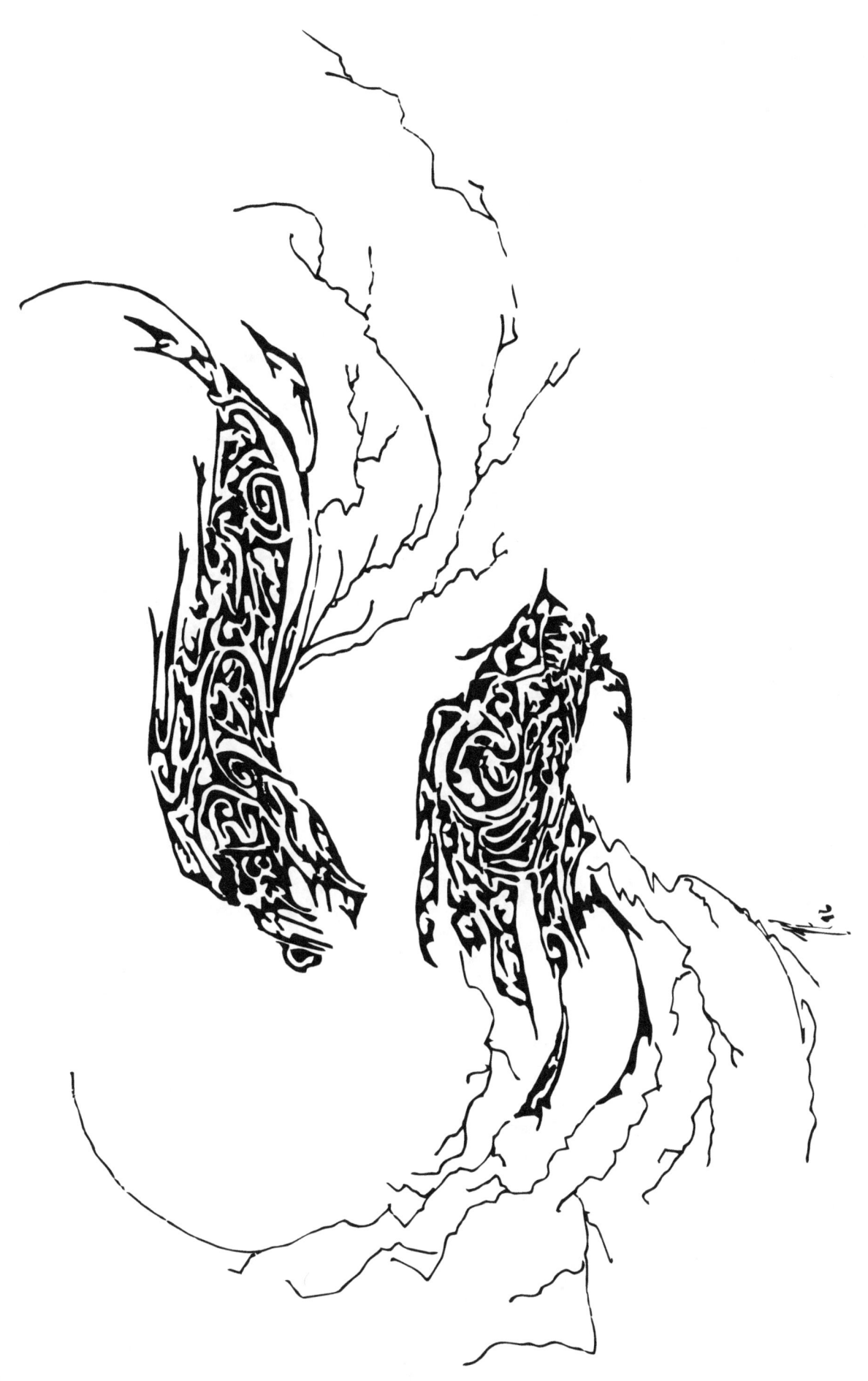

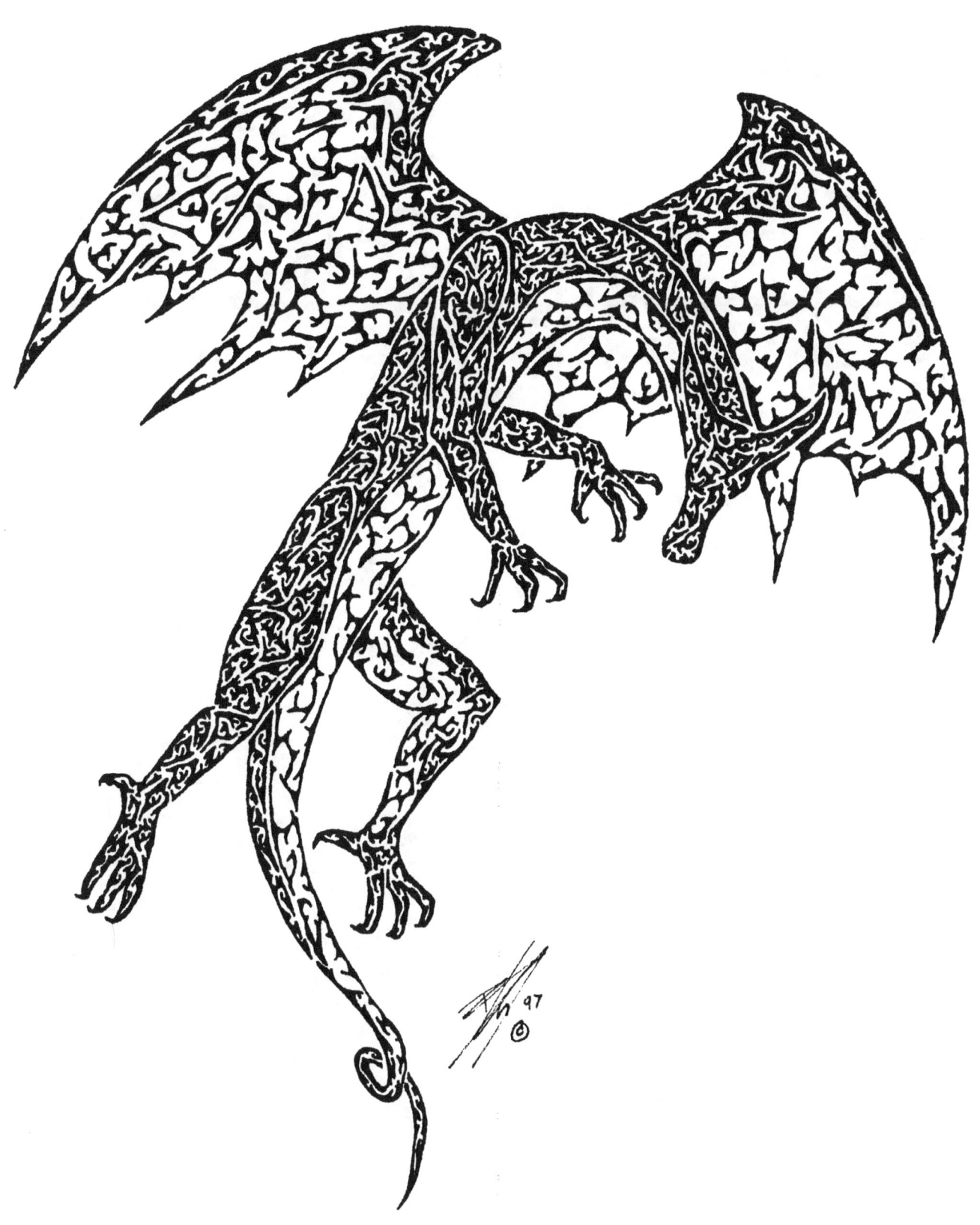

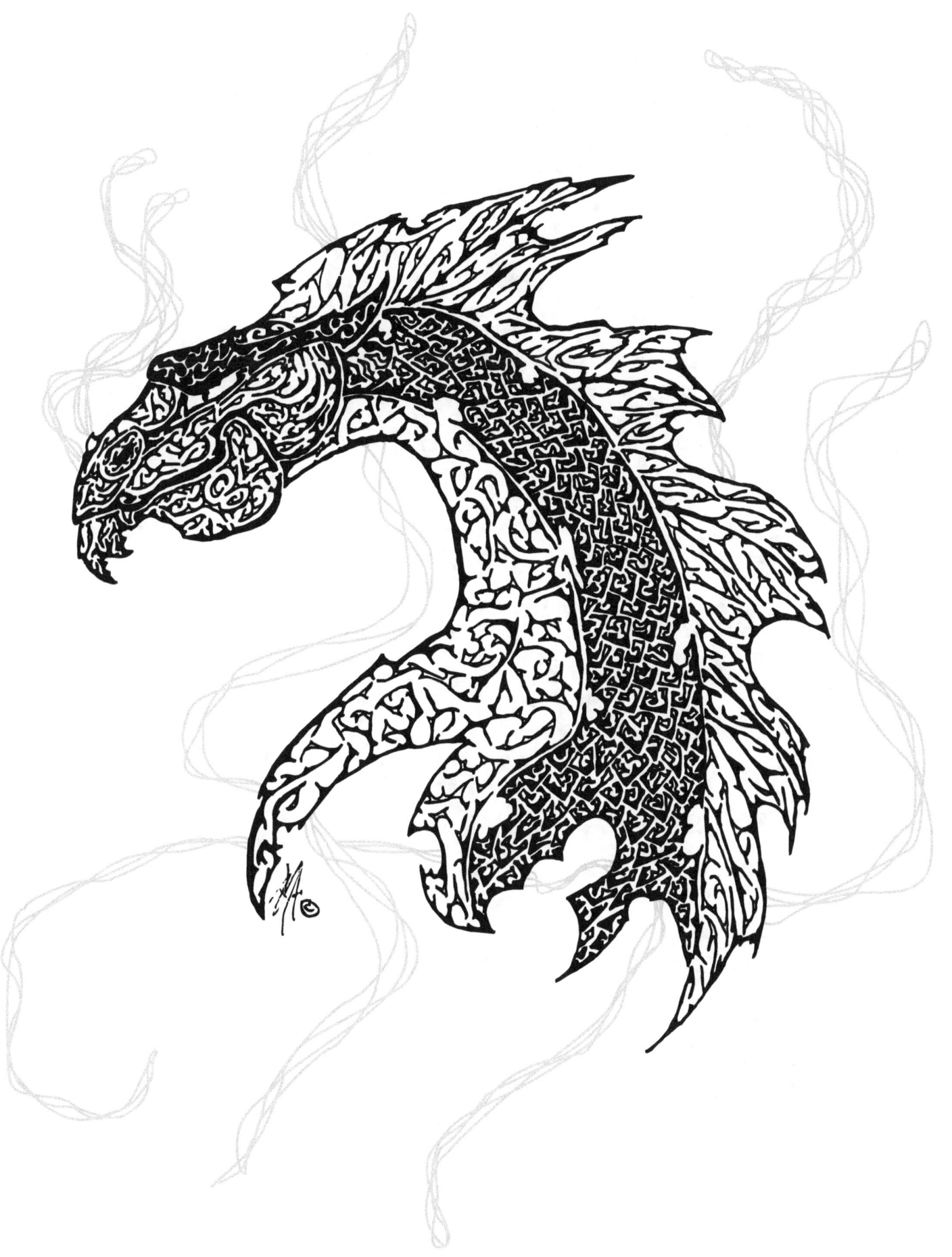

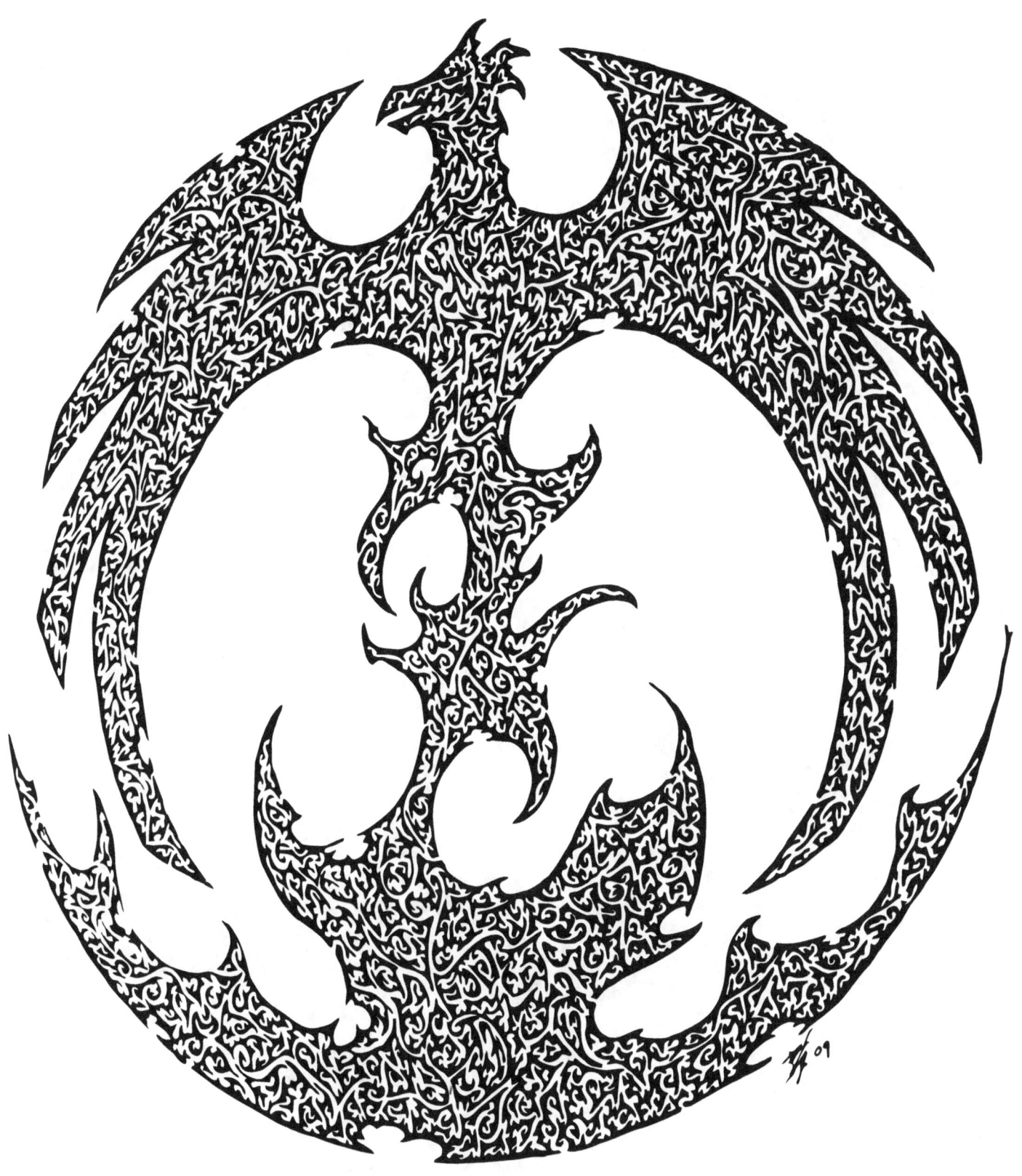

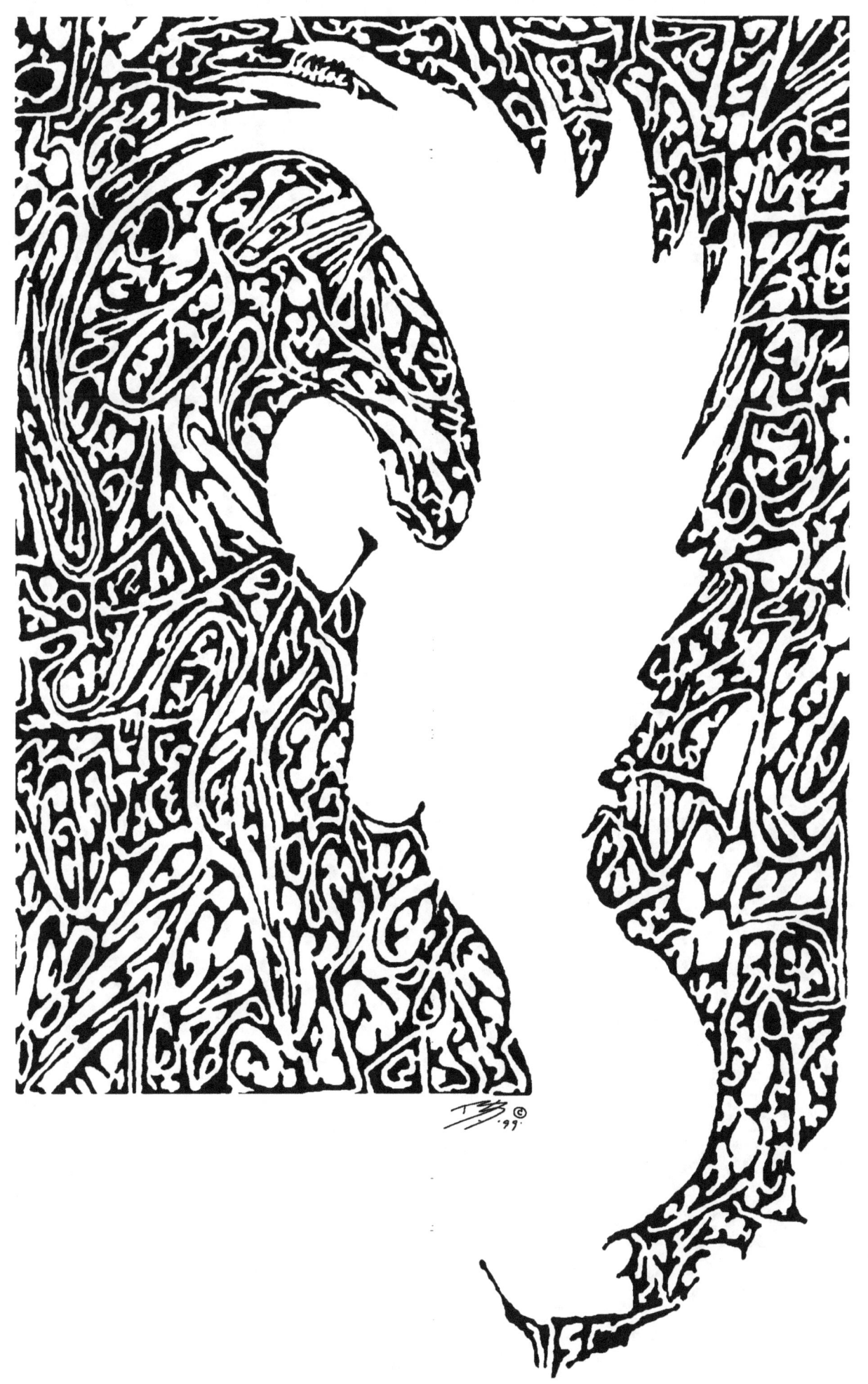

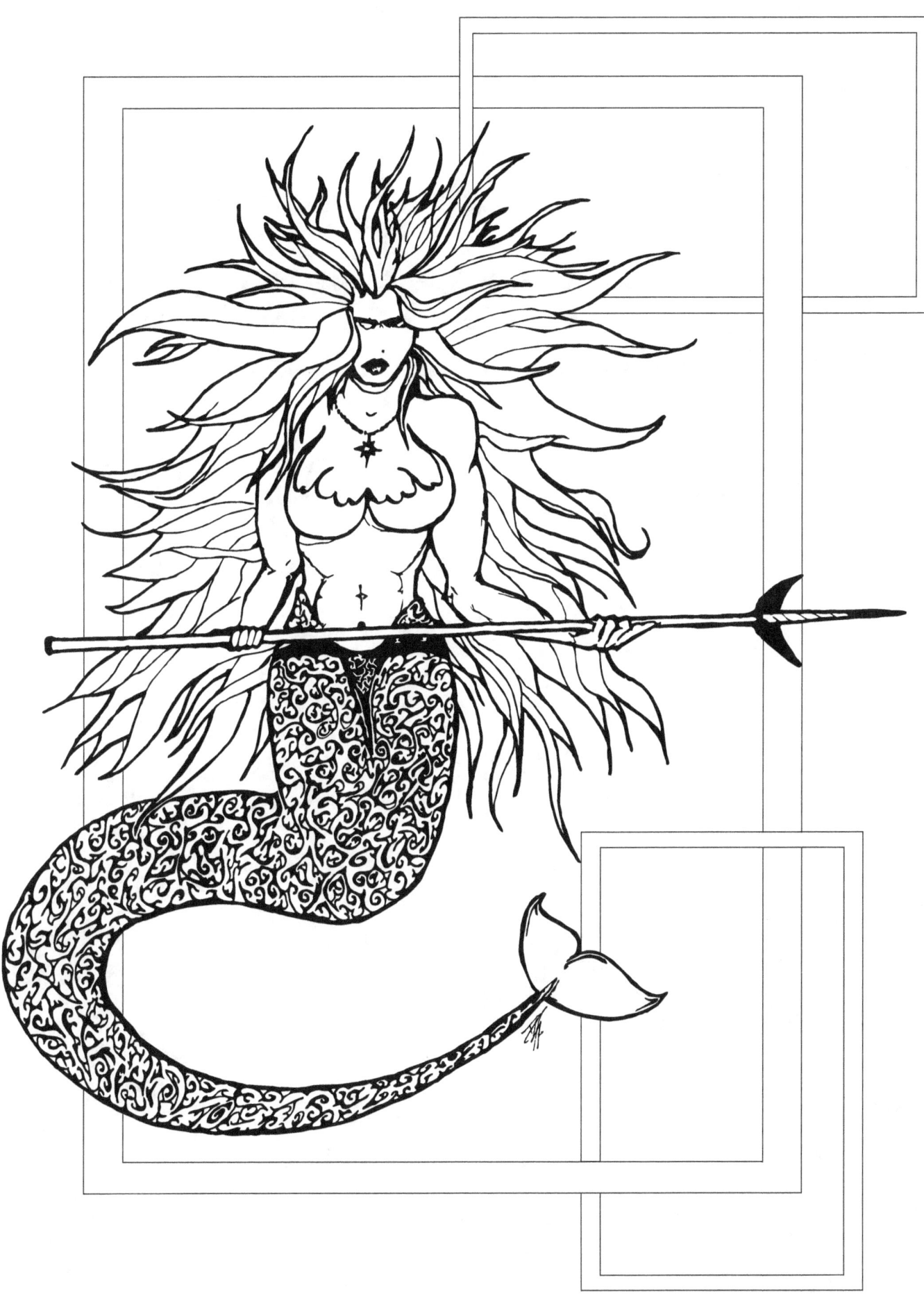

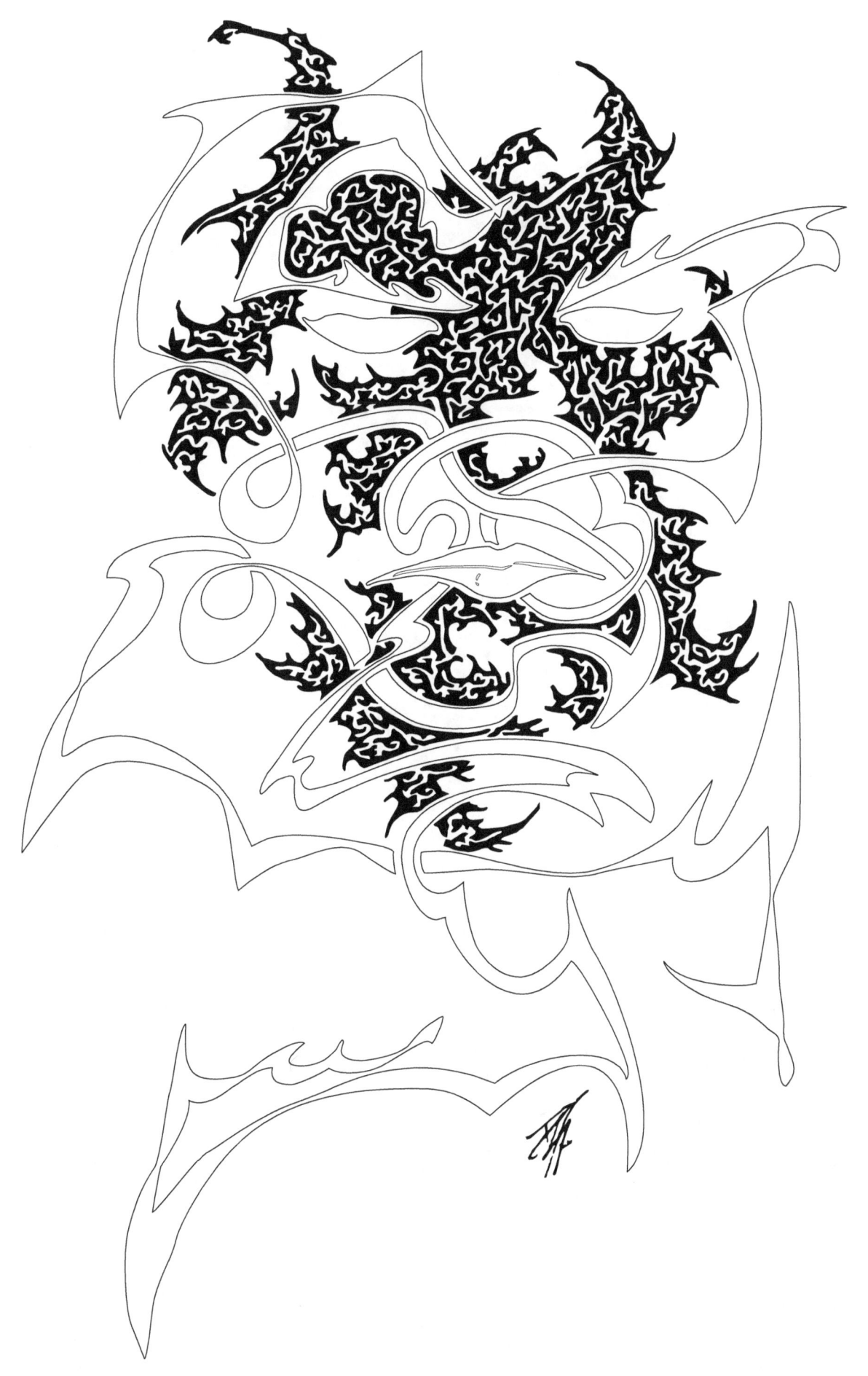

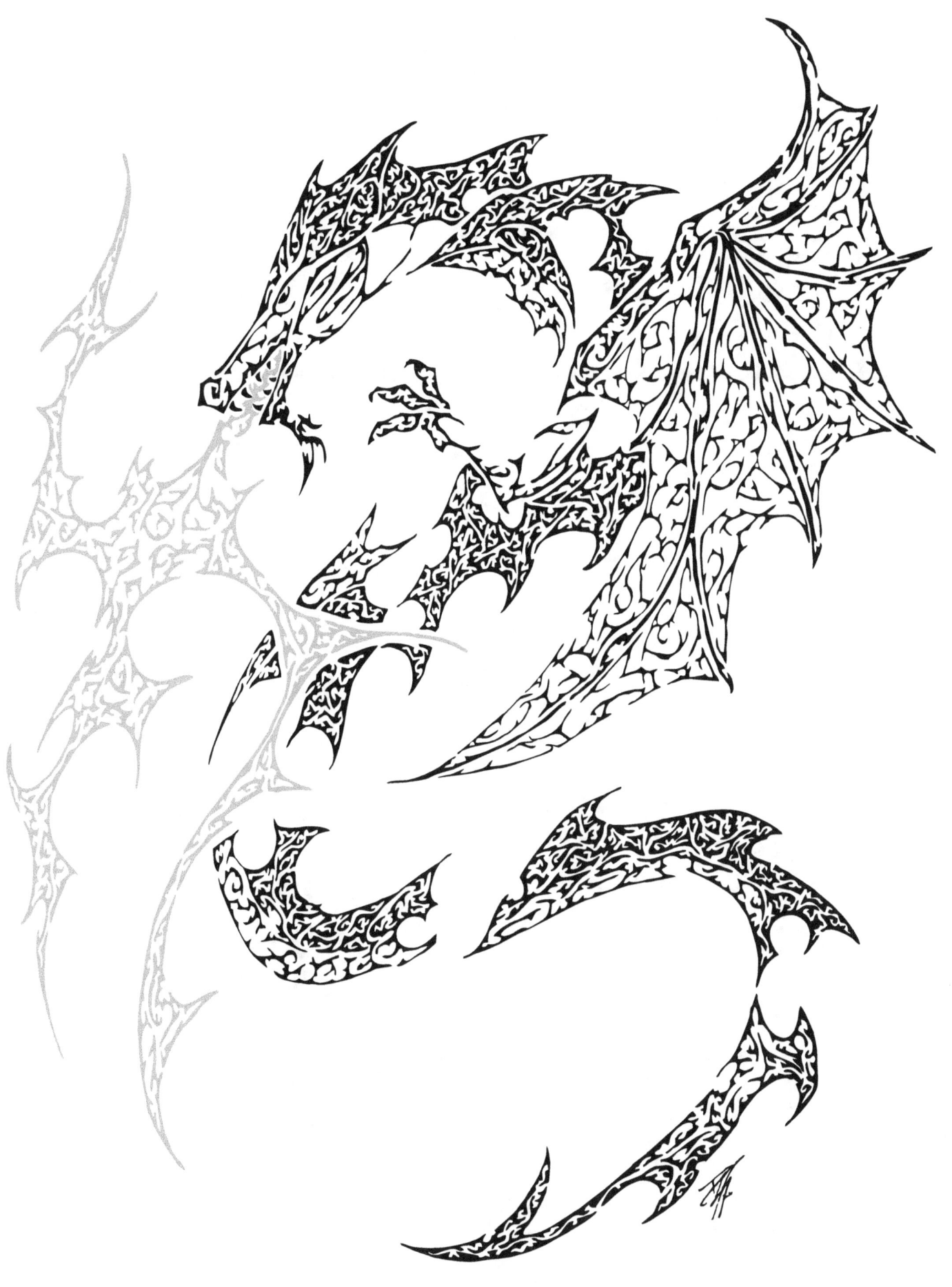

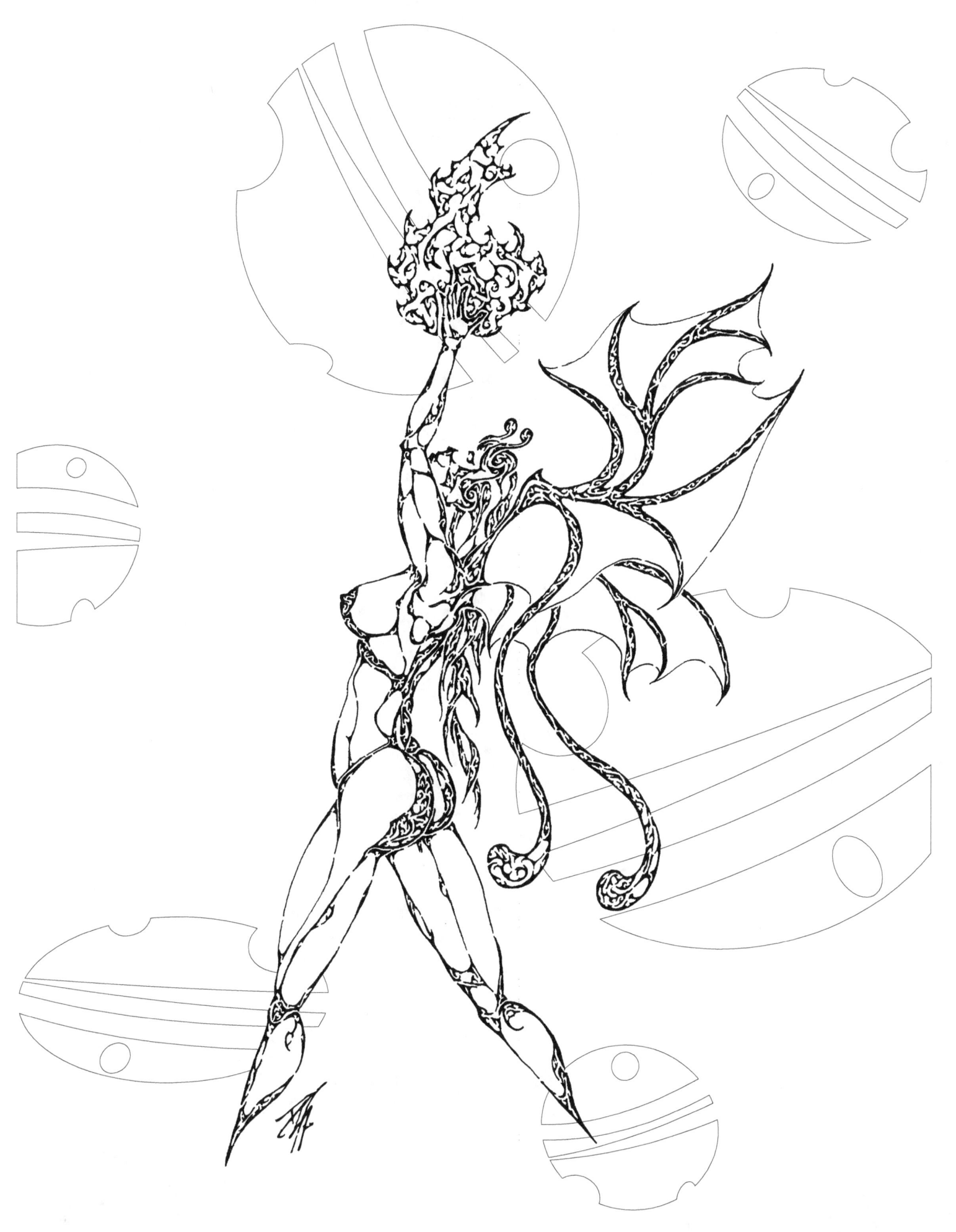

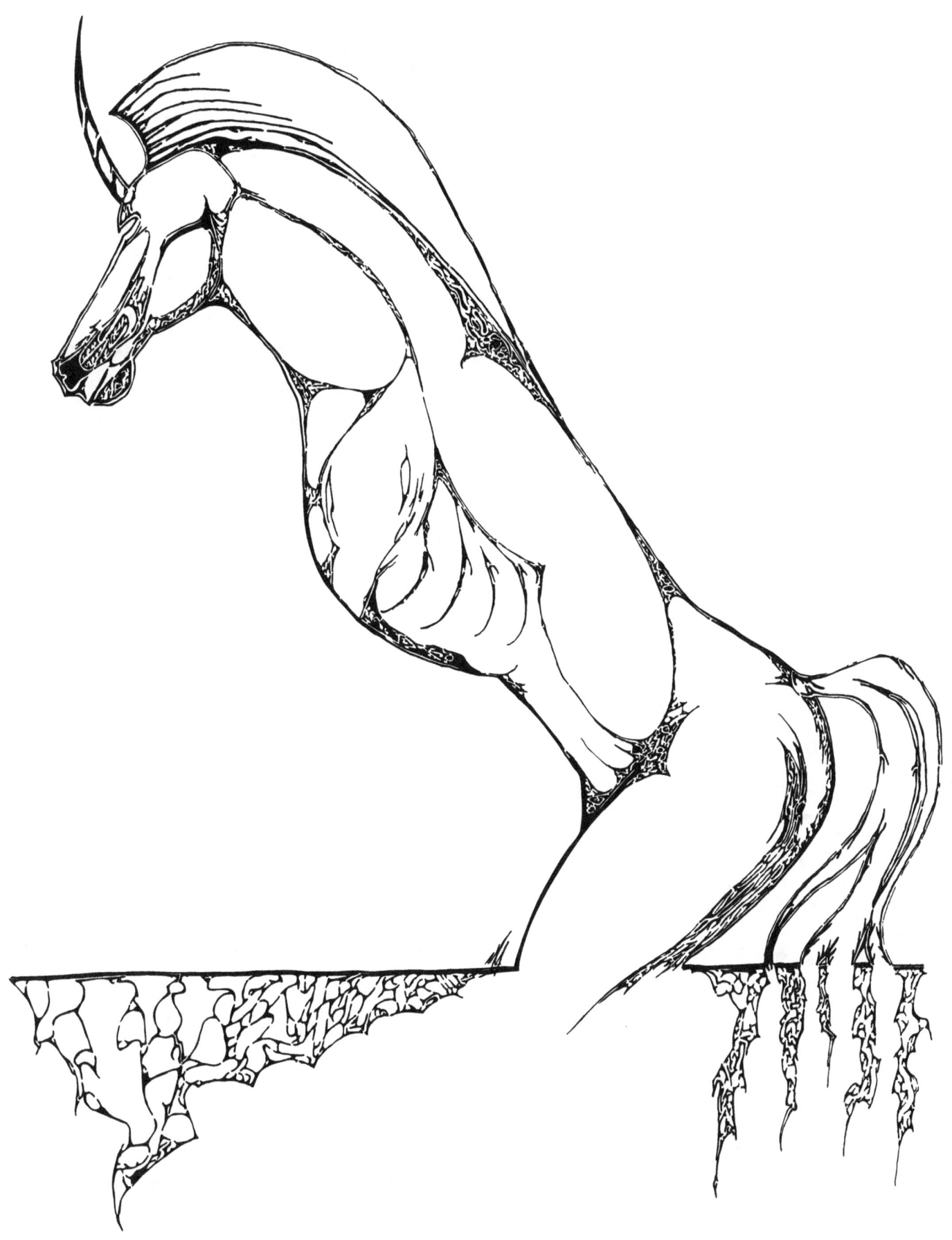

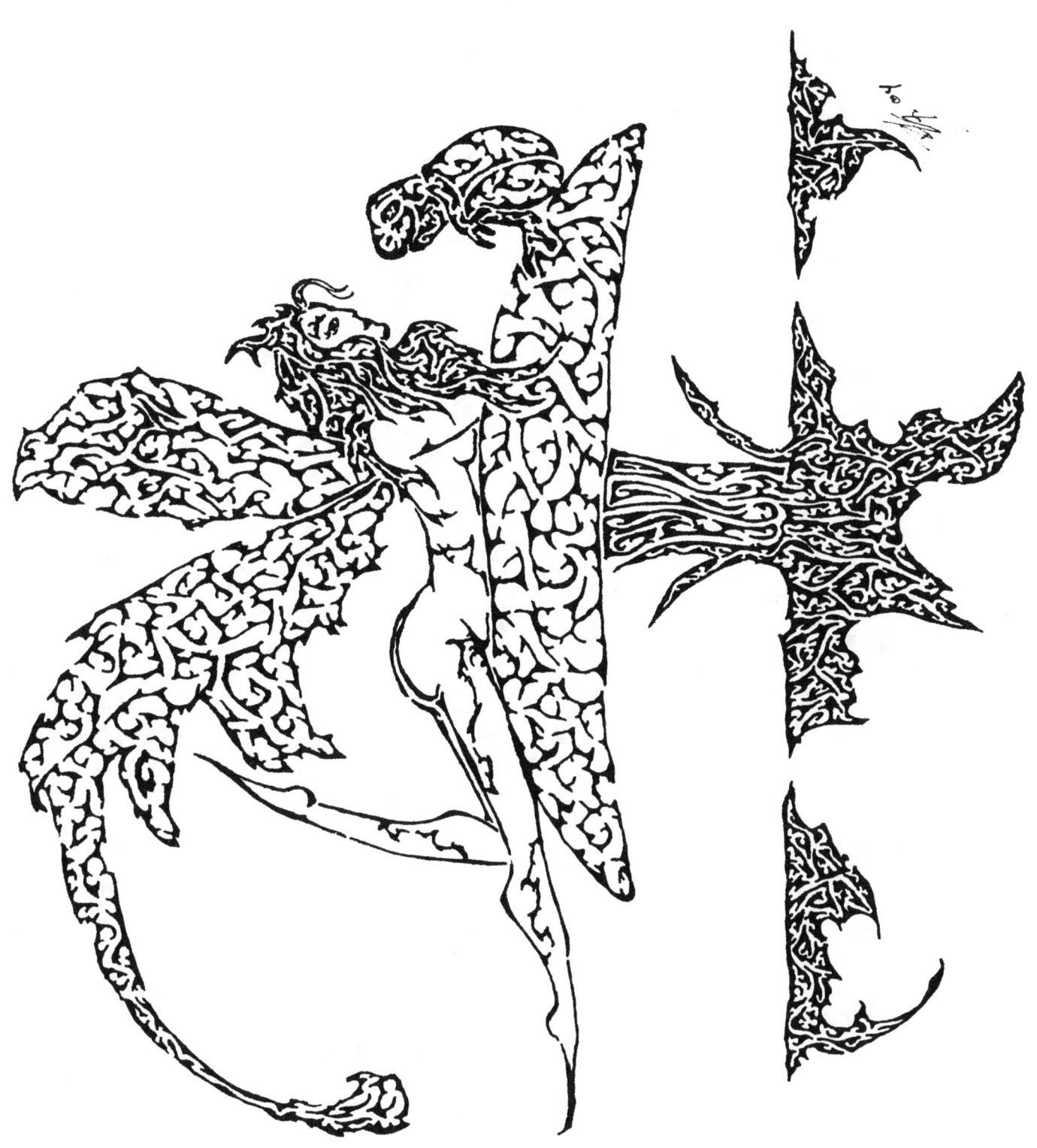

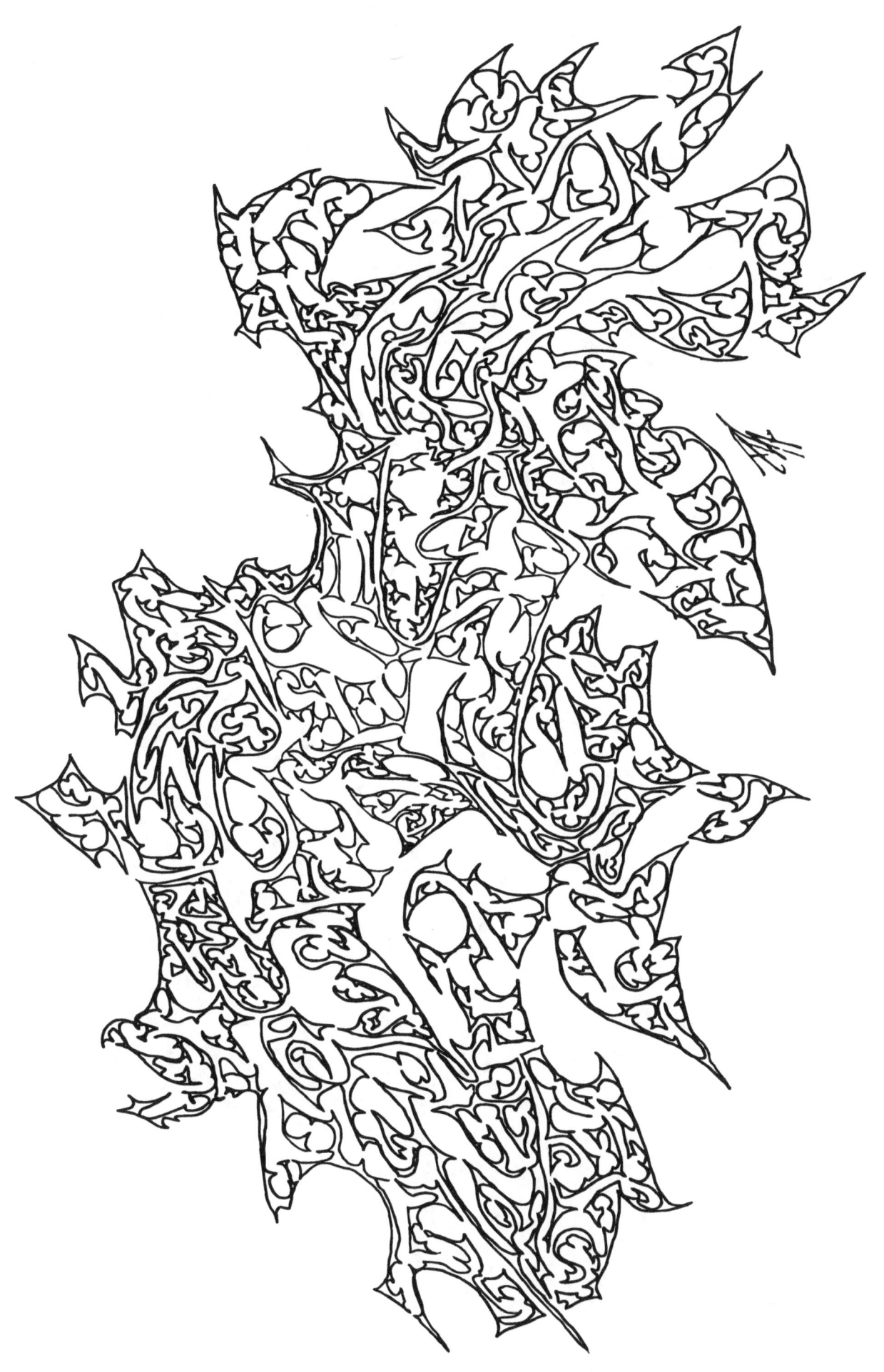

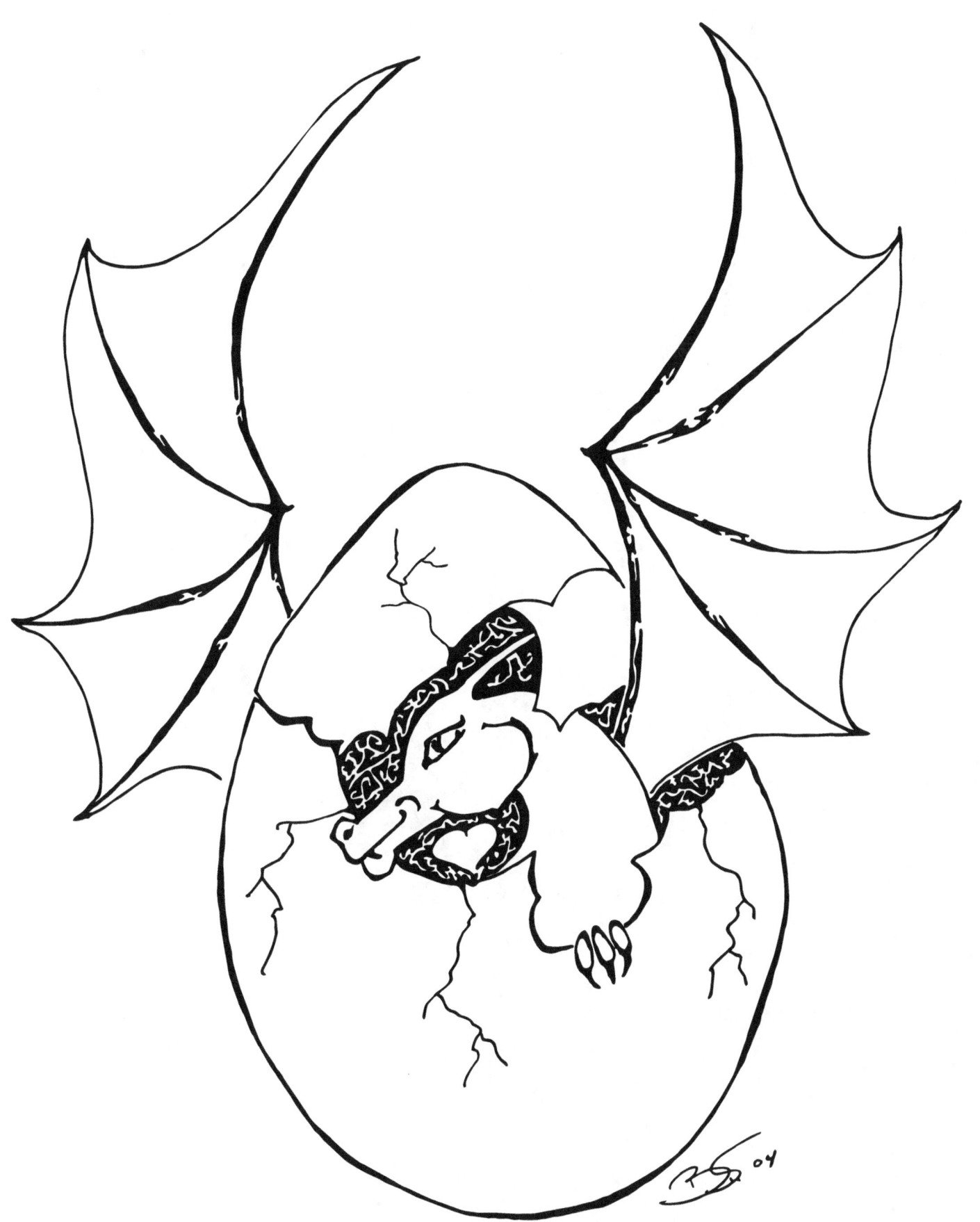

A page to test your crayons, markers, pens, pencils, watercolors on to see how they will bleed thru the paper.

A page to test your crayons, markers, pens, pencils, watercolors on to see how they will bleed thru the paper.

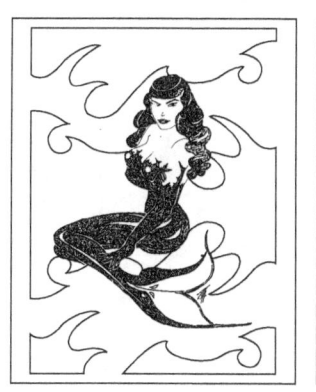
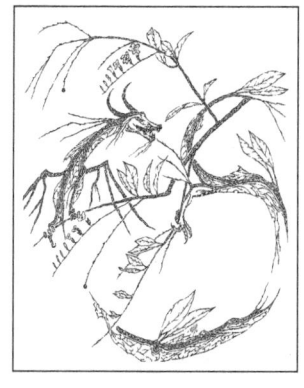
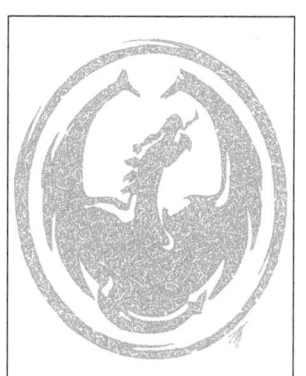
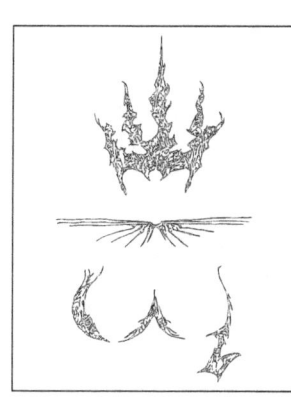

Part of the:
Inspired Art
Coloring
Books
Series

by Brian Scott

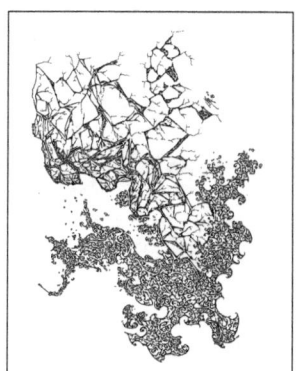
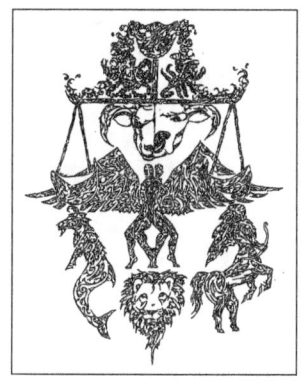
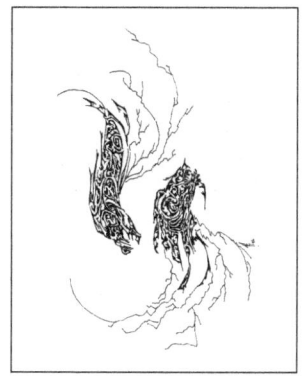
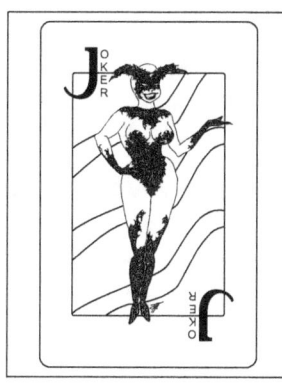
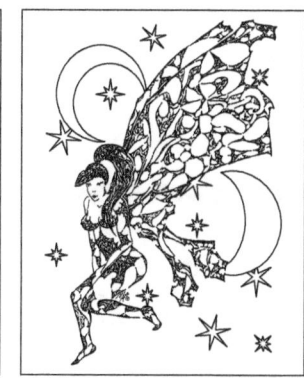

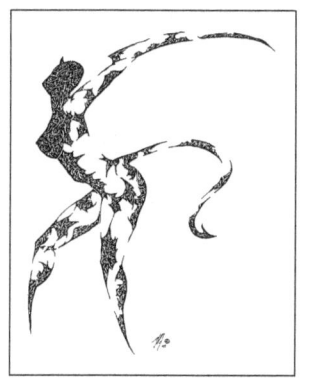
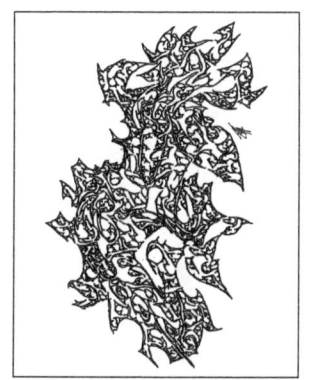
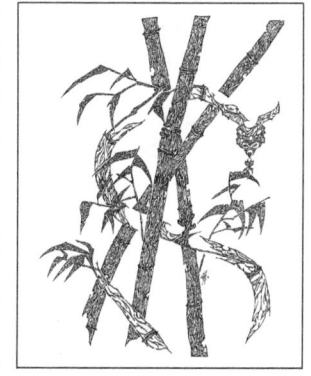
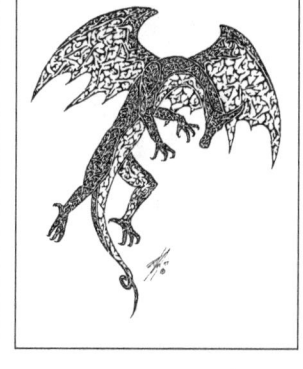
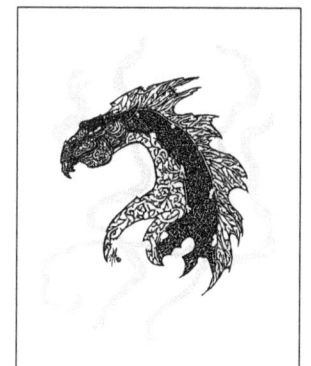

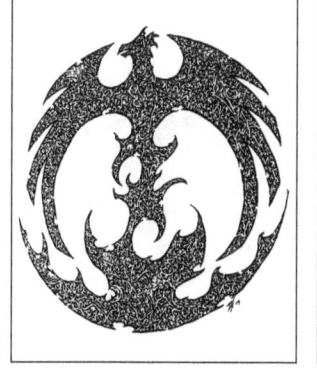
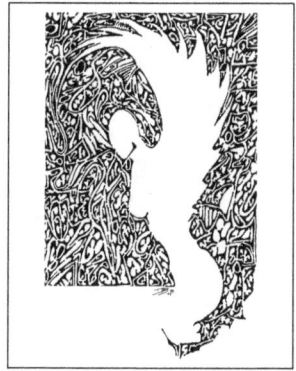
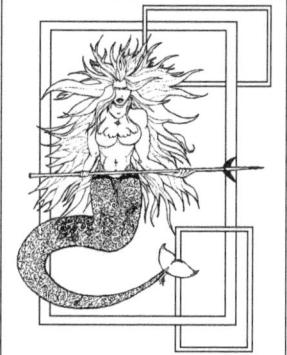
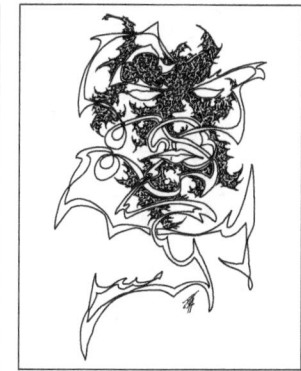
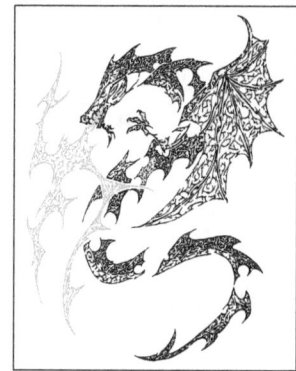

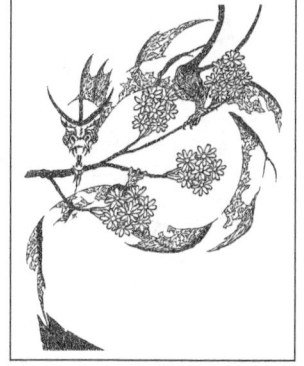
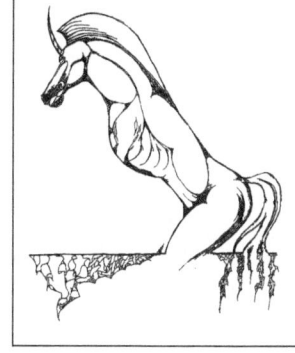
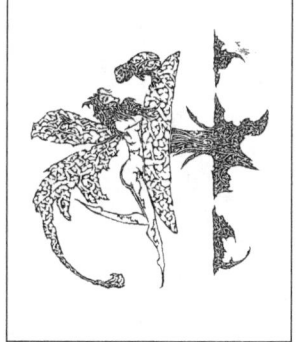
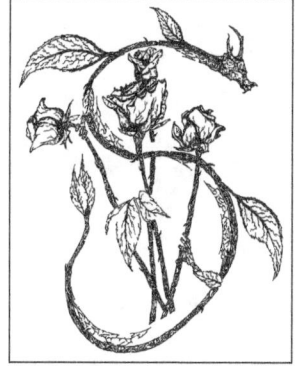
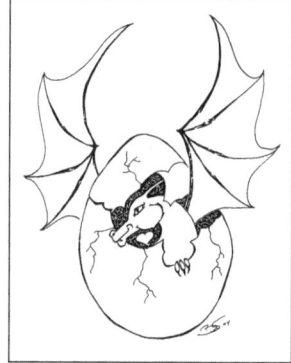